AFTER ESTRANGEMENT

AFTER ESTRANGEMENT

Poems by Molly Bendall

PEREGRINE SMITH BOOKS
SALT LAKE CITY

First edition
95 94 93 92 91 5 4 3 2 1

Copyright © 1992 by Molly Bendall

Published by Gibbs Smith, Publisher, Peregrine Smith Books,
P.O. Box 667, Layton, Utah 84041 (801) 544-9800

Design by Kathleen Timmerman

Cover photograph: Man Ray, *Kiki (Noir et Blanche)*, 1926.
Gelatin-silver print, 6 3/4" x 8 7/8".
Collection of the Museum of Modern Art, New York.
Gift of James Thrall Soby.
Copy print ©1992, the Museum of Modern Art, New York.

Photograph ©1992, the Man Ray Trust/ADAGP—Paris/Artists Rights Society—
New York.

Photograph of Molly Bendall by Karen Fish

Printed and bound in the United States of America

Library of Congress Cataloging-in-Publication Data

Bendall, Molly.
    After estrangement / Molly Bendall.
        p.   cm. — (The Peregrine Smith poetry series)
    ISBN 0-87905-467-0 (pbk.) : $9.95
    I. Title. II. Series.
    PS3552.E5384A69 1992
    811'.54—dc20

                                                    92-8614
                                                    CIP

for David

*. . . church-bells started their work
on the tawny evening while goodbyes
were being said to the mask-maker
at her gate.*
—Elizabeth Bowen

CONTENTS

I

II

III

IV

I

THE VISITATION

Perhaps I can deliver you.
Here is a diagram and a video tape.

How can I consider?
You're wearing a lavender robe
and there's a sleep mask pulled up on your head.
You're a divorcée.

What would suit you better?
Black flannel, pearl buttons—
don't hesitate—silk belt?
There will be no pasture of regret;
the terms are in your best interest.

How will it take effect?
I'll sit in a night club with black oval tables . . .
Your finger lifts a matchbook with
a single initial embossed on the cover.
A painting hangs behind me: an annunciation
taking place under a parasol on Long Island Beach
and across a cloud reads,
"I am the immaculate conception."

You cannot say for sure
not having visited that country.

On the contrary, I've spent summers
on a house deck with folding chairs,
scented candles, and a dusk that persuades
even the most single-minded.

You're faltering again.
I'm offering you this jar filled
with ether.

Do I fill it with insects
for my nightstand?

Between you and the other black
chair you'll find squat glasses
of flaming liqueurs that burn blue.
The orchestra will change tempo
when you're most comfortable.

Don't scold me.
I know the furniture's in disrepair,
but this is *progressive passion.*
It does break a previous vocabulary.
                You do speak low
and in various voices?
And I want to ask, is there
a wistful phase that follows?
If so, could I stand under a tree
with my jar as a luna moth
spreads itself
on the birch for the night?

> More decorum you want,
> but you could speak French
> (if you concentrated)
> for a mild onslaught
> on a polished body.

Maybe a little false—only for now—
until I can unbless myself and believe.

> Your idea of faith
> is leaving for the afternoon
> with the washer on "delicate"
> expecting to come back and find
> the clothes soft and understated.

If that room simply lies
right in front of me,
will they play on until I get there?
Will the stage floor have that black finish
too slick for stillness or good balance?
Don't go and leave me
with no expectations, no corsage.

WAITING

She takes a different route
when she goes out this night for cigarettes.
Her flat is disturbing because of the mice
and her toothache.

She doesn't even consider anymore
who would ever marry her.

•

Which stroke do we use to get from here to there?

For me the summer evenings are as indistinct
as his comforts have been lately.

•

"Will you turn the pages
as I play?"
                    He kisses her hair,
"It's too late . . ."

•

. . . the year Susan came to stage a ballet for us.
She'd been somewhat of a star. (I have a photo of
her from 1958—she smirks in a parti-colored costume.)
It didn't mean so much then, but
she put her hand
                    on my partner's shoulder
with a strange, violent grace.

•

A detour to the trestle was on this route, and
from it, she points to houses of a few friends.
The wind pulls the docked boats below Canal Street;
the wind tore a paper sign from a building.

•

One night he told me of the women in Osaka—he'd
been on leave, finally after four months—that
particular one in a black robe with gold leaves
who bathed him.   her collarbone   porcelain edge
    a pipe she put in his mouth   when he moved
his leg   her skin   his lip cut from her nail

•

"Did you ever say prayers?" she asks.
"On nights when I was told a compelling story."

•

The character, Lisette, slides her full blue skirt
more towards her to leave room for him on the bench
                    and lowers her head the other way.

•

Vinegar, avocados, potatoes, vermicelli in her arms
as she leaves the all-night market. In the window,
even at night, even with the pink of the street
lights, her expression shows fatigue.
She gloats over it.

•

After the reception for friends she feigned
his accent, "Everyone has an assigned shape:
hexagon or ellipse and we all fit into a huge mosaic
like your bathroom floor."

I push another glass toward her.

•

"You see," she tells him, "there's this trip
I have to make."

•

*I was alone. It was the evening and there was
a full moon over the sea. The wives of the
fishermen were, in procession, making a tour of
all the ships, carrying candles and singing what
must certainly be very ancient hymns of a heart-
rending sadness. Nothing can give any idea of it.*

FIVE MASQUES FOR THE BODY

1. Misery Loves

Summer began, first in his hands then
in his voice. A weak breeze barely passed
through his fingers. *Ask me again to the shore.*
I had told him once, such smells are here
like custard with nutmeg, not too salty.
We drank from glasses in small sips and carried
traces of the mackerel sky with us,
even if we didn't know what the weather was.

We had what you'd call a wordless arrangement.
When he stood at the door anxious with phrases,
I doubted them as lightly as I could.
Desires of everything dried with the day,
and I gave him one of my girlish looks
as if I had nothing else to offer.

2. For a Chinese New Year

Four years ago you brought me cloth and thread
and now you want me to make a folksong?

The dead woman you long for—
all I can do is hum in the gathering rushes.

You've sworn off drinking until the New Year.
At least that was what you said earlier.

I cannot rest even with the curtains drawn.
The fishermen's low fires keep me awake.

Now, when we slide onto the floor,
my flesh crawls with spectators.

I sit on the stoop in the middle of the gardening.
Shamrocks are a lighter shade than before,

and pollen falters on the stairs and roof.
It carries part of me away.

3. On Stage

This was how it was . . . you have a wife
—prettier. My name is in your mouth.
You've planned it all with the music—
these familiar limes and salt.
My shoulders tense up, the lighting's not there.
You: "one April there was a passion."
Me: "so unexpected it could have been right."
Don't you recognize me anymore?
You argued my side for a few moments.
Which one of us leaves first?
There's a rumor: you play it out, then I.
Far away, you've taken my waist in your hands.

4. Pastoral

No, I realize my stubborn side,
how I've neglected our room, the window sills.

My daughter watched the knobby-kneed calves
at the fence as if she'd never seen them.

It's rare for you to give her a gift
—she's not yours. I hear her whisper to herself.

We shucked the last of the corn.
The silks are weightless in my hands.

I know you will go on working
as quietly as a person can.

The wild roses are at it again.
You probably didn't notice so late in the day.

I want to grow my hair long.
Then I could ask you to braid it for me.

5. Sacrament

Secrets fling out of us to corners
of the room. There's really
nothing between us, but frailties.
I never thought you could go on so.
I say, it's morning and we must redeem
ourselves. Feed me eggs and toast. I'll hold
your cup up. Trust me. And you
so gently . . . How do you know?
I pass you the flawed pitcher,
the sun closes in on your chair.
Each drop of semen is a small gesture.
Certainly, it *is* that simple.
I lie back down. Won't you?
Winter leaves me, half-dazed.

INVITATIONS TO SPRING:
LETTERS WITH ELIZABETH

Dear M—

For a few days now, I've watched
one of the other guests
on the beach with her daughter.
They rush by me unaware and chase
a ghost crab into its hole.
The mother picks up her frantic, gawky pace,
leaving the girl, who concentrates then stoops
to pick up a *bleeding tooth* and *moonrises*.
Her mother turns with one collar side up
and in her usual chant says, "Leave some."

This woman brings much to bear
on what she proclaims as her home.
She places dried weeds and such,
festively but discreetly, in the rooms
with airy light. I listen: the birds
she loves so well in their opalescent greens
stammer almost sweetly.
In this boarding house I'm like any other
guest who's been away
and is not immediately welcomed back,
and I can't bring myself to call on her
in the shallow hours of midday.

Once I heard, as the girl napped beside her,
the woman singing
a not-quite-familiar Gaelic lullaby:

> *Hush! the winds roar hoarse and deep!*
> *Where they roam, where they roam*
> *Sister seeks the wandering sheep,*
> *But baby sleeps at home.*

I waited for other verses,
but she hummed them mostly,
filling in with her own words:
"shells" and "purses" and "Brother travels
a long ways off," for the parts
she couldn't remember.

If I've gone on too long,
you must forgive me.
I do plan to visit before
the month is up—
I will not be much trouble and
a not-too-elaborate room would be fine.
So if I can gather myself, I'll come
to follow spring through,
and its difficult triumphs, with you.

Dear E —

I would like to tell you how the alyssum
brocades the pieces of quartz bordering my garden,
and how the faithful breezes assure me
that loss does not perpetuate,
but for me to strike this pose
would be too unusual.
I want to plan a blustery day for your visit.
Could I interest you in a small lunch
at the patisserie or a long walk outside?
Tell me, what else about these birds
belonging to the woman?
Does she call them stuffy English names
in her very formal voice?
If I had a fancy, tropical bird like hers,
I'd frighten it, hold its sleek feathers,
then give it unexpected flight.

I look forward to our outings
and to your wild and fruitless bouquets
that I should like to put in inappropriate places.
On the especially humid days
I'll probably wear that awful turquoise camisole
that you said makes me look like a catalog girl.

And about the woman you saw —
I might ask her for a dance together,
(as I would you) briefly, never as partners,
a single spiriting dance, at the height of the season.

FOR LOUISE BOGAN

We are not content
to eat dusty bread.

Odor of hot trees
and mocking orchards—

I couldn't give them
to you anymore

than you could give me
the rest of your sweet

fields and unstrung leaves.
(Is that too baroque?)

Edges of night songs,
strangers that leave, once.

The invitations
are flawed, and somehow

are, just for the heart,
terribly invoked.

We'll cast a screen with
gentle syllables.

They are unfaithful,
but we can't abandon them.

It's a lonely blow.

LAUGHTER AND DIAMONDS

Queasy during our late walk
after the theatre, we got our bearings
by the turret in the distance. She and I
spoke of Nicholas—all that lovemaking
and what is there to tell about it?
"There's something about his neck
that's like a woman's," she said.
We passed by a close group
and gave half-smiles
at their old-world fidelity.
"I guess I was captivated by his small bones."

We coveted together
the poverty of his wardrobe.
Many nights as he studied
by oil lamp, we took turns
feathering him, occasionally coaxing
him to photograph us, and later
to paint in the color.

That night, I returned to his place
following my fragile shadow along
the splintery banister, listening
to her taxi pull away.
He slipped off my leopard coat
and lynx muff in his book-dark room—
"You shouldn't mix your beasts." he said.
Oh Nicki, lui, cher, liebchen!
I vowed to him, *his* head on *my* cameo.

She had left graciously,
buttoning her jacket with self-regard,
knowing she and I would replay it afterward
and imitate him as masseur and long for
the cream of his vocabulary.
Our delicate origami—
floating swan, empty teapot, he and I, she and I.

Until . . . I came home too early
in the afternoon. She, naked
except for my lace shawl,
slid his lizard belt from its loops,
and on the rug where she lay,
on two woven blossoms,
the indiscretion of their brandies.
She was telling him
her silly story of the geisha
who kept pet crickets in intricately carved pagodas
and trained them to be silent.
What he had loosely possessed
he regained now
with each accommodating reply.

She and I were once
on the brink of fortune;
standing behind the door, I remembered
with each bureaucratic minute
what she'd said,
". . . later you lovingly examine the facets
of regret, then you simply wear it
so it will be seen."

II

Nothing is so striking as the disparity between her many likenesses; and nothing so eludes portraiture as ecstasy.

—Marianne Moore on Anna Pavlova

PAVLOVA: ELEMENTS OF EVENING

1. The First Article of Faith

He's amazed at what I might add
with my neck or fingers.
If I could pull off this most spectacular,
buoyant curve—its very peak, the radiance
of our blue saucers thick with reflection.

(Not to give in to such *easy* alchemy.)

I'm touched by his full-handed complaints.
When I follow them,
the pianist, I often observe,
rustles her sheets quite clumsily as if taking
half the blame.
"You're a mirror-flower.
Your eyes should follow the arc."
Tapping his cane to tempo,
"*chassé cabriole, chassé cabriole, soutenu, chainé, chainé*—
Oh Anna, too colloquial!"

Parts of my technique are still watery
and some ask to whomever,
"Is her back not strong enough?
Perhaps she's just not determined
to try the exquisite tricks of the Italians."

I want my best possession to be a string of beads
cast in shell-blue, each one like a room
I could enter without really leaving the last.
And I say, as he pulls my sash, "Cream and yellow,
sort of weasely isn't it?"

"Not on you, never, dove-tail," he says.

On the Maryinsky stage I watch the leading role,
her entrée; she waltzes in like an amethyst
and yearns coyly to soldiers in the box.
Shortly, my continuous turns approach—
a thin, unending row of metallic snaps.
I pull my phrase free of its pleats and gathers
and after, there
remains a terror in its inevitable motif.

2. Hotel of the Black Swan

I tell you I've been strung with weighted bells
but enough with foreboding, our suite is waiting.
Once there, I pick up the obligatory vase and vintage fruit.
Ready to linger over borsch, perhaps,
then sherry, I try to convince you by insisting *she*
curried favor by complimenting me.
She performs with old-schooled stiff joints,
and her arms, here and there,
share nothing but bracelets of cowardice.

You invite the concierge to open
our heavy drapes where, beyond,
the violet trees are night-shy,
in spite of the distance.
Consoled by the sweep of branches
and the ultimate satisfaction of a rivalry,
I toast to cobras from our Egyptian nights,
and looking below, we translate a slow herd of sheep
into a quiver of remorse.

Four notes deep in the autumn mania,
I take in the view: slopes hooded with clouds,
cottages appliquéd on our valley.
I get lost in this sympathetic psychology
that slowly diminishes

revealing little to me, but a bit of scorn.

3. Parisian Love Letter

Dearest,
I know it must appear to you
that I'm on a grand mission for pearls.
If you were here
I would so love to be unrolled
from the Turkish carpet;
I'd have on a layer of fur then beneath that,
my off-the-shoulder tunic.

What could be fancier? (As yet unconsummated . . .)
But I entice myself in a black organza gown
with four poufs and right away
I can quote you with your air of childish rarity.
Mastering a sleight of hand, last night
I extended from my silver egg cup
in a downpour of pink light.
Finned with crepe and lace, I would've persuaded
the blackest Russian, sure.

I dote over this quilt, sewing daily,
each of its little pillows, a medallion, a scrap
from a variation, and I sleep with it
like a charm or a wordless book to read in my insomnia.
(You're in your sparrow-feather-brown. We wander
to our cherub fountain,
its base cluttered with leaves.
They are bits of fluted paper
from our chocolates. Let's go back.)

4. Renunciation

Nine P.M. has its signature, looped with invisible knots—
much bravura initially, then spun
more sentimentally.
Even though its yellowish light gilded
the ribbons and cummerbunds, I'm sorry to say
it falls short of a historic place.

I could only complete the role when I believed
there was no melodic horizon
or when I failed my promise
not to glance at whatever storms
might travel with me abroad.

Giselle loosens her skirt from her fingers
and drags a sword in circle around her feet
then waits for Albrecht to catch
the lily she throws over her head.

You take me from the night's encounter
arousing me with anecdotes of Indian spices
mistaken for aphrodisiacs, as you unfold
your not-to-scale map of the city.

Would that I could comply, if I could see
the combinations as nothing more
than a faltering scheme.
But the darkness of these wind-blown strands
is underlined by such cool deliberation.

5. The Mirror

She mustn't attend solely to her tiara
of wintry trees. She hides
her fan, an undone chain of overlapping scenes.

I can foretell the end as I watch her.

When I know that arm means
a river   a river for waterbirds,
when I dwell on her sanguine skirt
speckled with black as it opens into a blood-glow,
then the unnatural has overcome and taken charge.

On her widow's walk, recalling her former lover,
she folds the fan—that sequence is cushiony,
conducive to headiness—
and everything after the elaborate bridge
will be sleek and serene.
I saw her in a gothic glade
wearing a forbidden aigrette,
and she dressed her table with bowls of lilac . . .
and inside these arenas
she saw herself, again, abashed
at the uneven wheels of her carriage.
This combed garden belongs to someone else,
she exclaims and vows to pretend
once more to do something she knows
won't be reconciled.

6. Ecstasy

When I was young, I learned quickly
my mother's satirical gentleness.
She loitered at my door
and I thought this posturing,
well, too familiar.
She wore a brooch pinned on the waistband
of her apron: a currant
buried in white icing.
Even the swan has a low threshold for sorrow,
and I couldn't make enough moments for distraction.
Busy in my shrine, cap-sleeved and sheathed,
I folded imaginary trousseaus.

My fever dream of swimming flowers
aggravated me; I blamed the wallpaper.
I remember many blessings for Mary
but when I learned to sip tea
from tiny cups, I thought not of her
nor of anyone but Taglioni
and her necklace casketed with ice.

Ah, she, my model for the heart.

Unlike Venus, who eagerly came
in her traces of foam on a whim,
she held her own in a final salutation
returning to the virtues of calmer waters,
too quiet to ask for
an arrangement of shells
or the bliss of an extra-long summer.

III

CONVERSATION WITH EVA HESSE

Where do you live?
    On the block with lots of 5's.
    The one with the glass doorway, the wavy glass
    and a one-sided shaky banister.
    All the houses are pressed together
    like boxcars, pulled by the Victorian
    on the end.

What do you say to your lover?
    Up came
    an Eighter from Decatur
    then he found her
    went around her
    but what do you care?

    I feel like my knees.

To what bakery do you go?
    The Ukrainian one with the pastries
    that have raisins like my mother's eyes.
    You're not always sure what's inside.

Where is the park you walk through?
    It has an ear in the lake
             And I imagine 14 legs under
    the surface holding it up.

    I wish it were indoors. I can't stand those
    outdoorsy sculpture gardens
    with big-leafed plants and trickles.

    You can't name a simple phallus
             unless it belongs
    to this body   body of water.

Is this piece finished?
    Too right and too beautiful,
    I'd like to do a little more wrong
    at this point.

    I called it stove-pipe dreams
    and then I sat all night wondering
    what to put inside the head
        later called it
    circumflexion   maelstrom

Does it speak?
    There's no fucking space—
    I put myself in front
        then behind this screen.
    Here, a stem comes out of the mouth
        a tired mouth.

How will you see it through?
    It must arrive
    without me.

A PAINTER OF DESTINIES

You said, "Come in to the light
that furs the wooden frame,
that makes the canvas porcelain."
It *is* here: the bottled music
of my likeness.
So I began to tell you how
the aromatherapy had been a failure,
but that, still, there were moments
of lucid temptations,
utterly tranquil in their strokes.
And I loved the threshold
I came to—came to dust,
the sworn chore I performed
with some panache—until my reward
was given to me
in my relatives' foreign
language, and I regressed
to loving bicycles.
But never once did I claim
settlement. Always,
I panned for topaz and took in
the unexpected visits
of music teachers, however silly
their watches were (the crystals
dramatized checkerboards and horsehair).
You've shown me the way to redo
my leaning gardens under mantles
and mutant sorrow,
grown stale in a studio like your own.
Yet after I saw the body
stripped for surgery
pining for tethered urns,
you told me, even while sitting
in the one delicate chair,
I must expect
only useless science in return.

CONVERSATION WITH FRIDA KAHLO

Who brought you up?
    I drank milk from a dark woman's nipple.

What are the colors of Coyoacán?
    mauve, pecan, ochre, lime

Where is the brown nurse?
    She's eaten the earth, roots branch from her limbs.

What's that on your dresser?
    A candied skull.

What shall I call you?
    Tehuana, she wears lace hoods while her husband
                has no shoes.

Where is your dress?
    It hangs there, wounded.

Is this your self-portrait?
    No, I've been miscarried.

Do you suffer?
    The deer's wounds bleed, but I am calm.

What do you want?
    They ask for airplanes, they are given straw wings.

LETTER

*I live like a plant, filling myself with sun and
light, with colors and fresh air.*

—Flaubert

From this window ladies' hats pass
on the street, reminding me of

hummingbird feathers scattered
by a gust haphazardly. Downstairs

the landlord's little girl pushes
pillows of dough with her rolling pin,

flour on her nose and ear.
She holds her apron strings

tightly in the corners of her mouth.
When she moves, her footprints will be there

in an *L* as she intended, surrounded by
a thin layer of sifted flour.

In the next room her older sister
practices her scales on the upright.

Music rises with the smell of burnt sugar.
Her feet rest lightly on the pedals.

This afternoon she'll go out—
her father frowning at the doorway.

She'll wear a hat, another blue feather to follow.

CONVERSATION WITH MARY CASSATT

Where have you been?
    Here, touching up the shawl   pinpoints of light
    through a straw hat   frying oysters   a bit of
    housekeeping.
    I'll see you again at Bachvillers under a better
    sky.

    The face has no animation but that I believe
    he does on purpose, he does not talk to his
    sitters.

What do you say to your sitters?
    Perhaps a few jokes about the English—they are
    such screws—I don't know how they manage it.

    Mother is well as yet, she talks of going south
    but I don't know if she will get off or not.
    The doctors don't wish her to go to Nice or
    anywhere on the seashore on account of her heart.

                        And all that's behind them
    and the boat is blue lake water.

    I could almost leave it as if that were all
    there were   lemon wedge   sugar bowl
    the apple green

Where is your father?
    I think he, for an instant, recognized Jeannie
    and the baby—
                    slight convulsions at the end.

    I know this one, he rides on the back of
    Isabella, her tail a swirling wave of chestnut.

    We've had such a dry summer here.

What do the children say?
>   The children are not awfully disgusted. It's
>   just ennui like when the heat is unbearable.
>   Of course I tell them, don't pout too much.
>
>   The little girl in the blue armchair was refused
>   and M. Degas even helped.
>
>   So you think my model unworthy of her clothes?
>   She in her moiré and moonlight jet, her untidy
>   nails, her copper hair.
>
>   I must take some of your nuts to Renoir who
>   suffers at times greatly, senile gangrene in
>   the foot.

What do you want?
>   I cannot understand a *personal* god. Almost
>   all my pictures with children have the mother
>   holding them, would you could hear them talk,
>   their philosophy would astonish you.
>
>   Bit by bit this woman surrenders
>   where the next color begins—
>   her pinkish orange robe, the child's buttocks
>   in the crook of her arm, one hand
>   holding the other wrist.

Where are you going?
>   Couldn't we (my brother and our friends)
>   breathe better in the field shattered with
>   poppies, a few cornflowers . . . ?

LATE SUMMER

I sat silently examining
the candle's apologies until
my dish came, an oval of lamb
draped with hollandaise
and fringed with parsley.
I told Jacqueline my ballet class
had been difficult,
and that we had to pose without
moving a bit—Madame insisting
it was good practice for the stage,
but I imagined being dead.
"Morbid, but instructive I suppose,"
she said, and went on about the party
I'd missed, "Therese was profiling herself
all over *everywhere*.
And your beau was there,
grinning with his fish teeth!"

I'd like to spare him
my real intentions,
but he wouldn't care anyway.
Only a few years ago
we spent our summer at the villa
and rowed out nightly
on our little pond, the moon
leaving a white road on the water.
I told him, "What I most want
is more *bijouterie*."
"Served on toast,"
he said, "I'm sure."

Then I thought of crystallizing
the isolation I felt,
or at least making it
as brilliant as that sun
ricocheting
from silver teapot to silver tray.

"I do want something
more for lunch," Jacqueline said
(she prided herself on being
able to order an omelet
in thirteen languages),
while the couple next to us
celebrated the color
of their sauvignon.

I told her what had impressed
me recently was the famous dancer
I'd met back-stage,
and how she wore a bodice
that had a small torn piece that
fluttered slightly . . .
It was like every nerve of
a lit lagoon or even like
an eyelid in restless sleep.
And I'd hoped
after seeing her that one smidgin
of pain was alleviated
because she was part of something
I'd never known,
such ardor and perfection.

CONVERSATION WITH ISADORA DUNCAN

How do you move?
    birds leaving water   mildly

What are your props?
    windmills   waves rising   columns   sky

What do you see there?
    the silhouette of a man sitting in an olive grove

Where are your children?
    when they call   gold leaves fall from their mouths

What was the dance you performed?
    the peasants plant their seed   I hold out my hands

What is death like?
    another dance   light falling on white flowers

What does the audience do now?
    laughter   uprising   I come at them headless

IV

STARLIGHT FROM HAVANA *(the 1930's)*

Standing center of the window's blue wishbone
    reflection, she made sure the goldfinches
and lawn birds were in perfect measure, and flirting
    with the door, pulled it almost shut.

On this long-awaited arrival day she was impatient
    for him to know their code of bird calls, and
again instructed him that the Cuban sun had a shy,
    at times belligerent manner, and "yes," she said,

"the crooning sky can be absolutely purple."
    She admitted she'd come to near-bewilderment
from napkin notes, the fits and starts of
    weekly letters. She'd sat against the radio

and listened to her ukulele friends and other sagas,
    writing to him with IOU attached,
"A boa of jacaranda for your neck,"
    and with this, a few stray petals.

They stepped out to their last night there
    in casino-red and her newly clipped hair just
meeting her collar. "Not another crude joke,"
    she protested, and with her ritual demureness

accepted an oblong turquoise pebble for each ear.
    The next morning from the heights of leisure,
they rose to their boat. "Say goodbye to Christina,
    goodbye 'Tonia. Send flowers, send charm!"

She left accompanied by coarse tropical rain,
    a moody dinner, and the recollection of her
brief promise to go back to an old pier where she'd gone,
    as a girl, to confess each mistake, each careless wish.

BALLAD OF PEACHES

Within our finely orchestrated
tableau, some of us
might gaze at her
to bring on the evening.
My uncle's poorly timed

toast rose and fell
as we welcomed his friend,
a business colleague,
and passed around
our hand-held motorized fan.

And when this friend met
her—my distant cousin—
I wished immediately to announce
my speculation
that this was the woman he would

have spoken to in the sub-tonics
of his nights. She led him
through our pavilioned feast
surrounded by flower beds, and they bent
to admire the miniature leaves of herbs,

and she plucked, for him,
a stem of thyme. Did others
know? He was an inconvenience, a stranger,
but a near-enough-scenario
for her.

And as I handed out
the frosted glasses, I longed
for the merest glimpse
at an artful ecstasy,
where the lawn was brushed felt,

the sky, blue clay
pressed on a board,
and the clouds slid
in between, like a gel
on a spotlight.

I wanted to be,
as she was, touched
then without words
at a nephew's delivery of persimmons
fresh from the yard's border.

"Already he's giving perishable
gifts," a great aunt exclaimed,
and my relatives on
their shady sabbaticals,
gossiping through hibachi smoke,

winked then turned back.
They looked her way.
A milky camisole scalloped
her tanned back, and I,
an apprentice

at glossy gestures
and night-time protocol,
was requested to do
the pouring. I slipped
around the lawn chairs in awe

as she told of her recent trip
to the South Seas,
how she'd been sick the whole way
(I imagine her leaning over
the boat, her legs trembling

beneath her culottes, and her hair
thrown over—already with nests
of grey). Then as she laughed,
the stranger committed blunders and
quite a faux pas: he compared her

to his pale canary . . .
The tranquil pause needed
rescue. And he thought all was surely
forgiven when she toasted to his bird
and applause disguised the moment.

No one took the opportunity
to notice that she led
him to the stuffy indoors,
and I was left to conjure.
Inhibited, I hoped for rain

or some sort of ruin
to bring them in closer view
as seed helicopters gave final spins
and lay on the white-draped tables
and the last outside

light faded,
leaving the glow of tigerlilies
with their lips peeled back
ready to say her name.
What could I

later recall of an episode
that I was not
a party to? During the half-hour
the two stayed in,
young cousins swiped sugared roses

from leaning cakes
and giggled into their hands
as they gathered
around my uncle's flourish —
a history lesson for their benefit.

She came out flushed on the stranger's arm
and pointing to the lanterns
in their starry semi-circle,
she said, "Oh, such possibilities
in the backyard of a three-story."

But I wanted to know
of a later time. How would I speak
of this nearly-typical July dusk?
After the pinks of shrimp salad
and the unpolished quartets?

With her assurance and approval,
I would say it was a "garden party"
embellished with mint leaves
in the iced teas, political lounging,
and the sins — only slight.

MEDIEVAL FASHION

The exhausted fire
left the chaotic fields.

How could they ever have yielded
fans of spinach, wheat, and gem-like beetles?
She glanced half-heartedly
at his tilted figure amidst the ash,
preferring to be engaged by a sublime white—
her gathered eggs in bowls and fallen flour.
Exalted by the lunar triptych
of the room's walls, she hummed
her own prayer-relic for everyone, especially
for her favorite rooster's bloody throat.

Her George was far that day,
and farther still, pink smoke
canopied the hedgerows miles
from the mill's passage. There,
he wondered which astral-tier had
brought cold, with no patience, to fall
on distant steeples and his own roof thatching.
The moon held her spades as the black
land of sprigs and knots remained
undone in celestial shadows
and forged bars of light.
He offered his own quarter-life
as it turned before him
and its certain wear
of nearby village histories
woven in all formality, all sacredness.

Spinning, Shearing . . .   Once, in a spell of the afternoon,
she and Catherine picked
blossoming cocoons from the branches
then made a tune for silk
and its extraordinary distance.
Holding plump bundles for her distaff
she discovered, quite by accident,
as she spun the floss between her fingers,
the spiritless grace of numbers.

Later she spoke easily of winters
to be reckoned with and of their modest
herd. What promises he had
as they stroked the rumps of sheep!
She hoarded his comfort-replies and,
silently, he counted on hesitant mornings
and the eternal chord
of her face near an open window.

In her pale chemise she began
to welcome him more elegantly
than even she had expected,
and helped loosen the criss-crossing laces
from his shins. They looked toward
the night, like those nights they dreamt
of lost kindred and profit-wishes
hundredfold, as the melancholy hush
of a weathervane against
the moon's thin horn brought
a dark-green twilight, and the Weaver
gingerly, painstakingly went on
with the luminous sky.

Incantation
for the soft
texture of linen.

The house she knew trembled with breath-
and-wave-motions as she walked toward
the briars and vines hanging awry
in the door's archway. He understood
without her divulging
the swift persuasion of illness that
had settled, and in the wake
of her staggering confusion
she inquired whether water boiled
in the Northern country.
Then he brought more broth to her bed.
"O let me tell you this tale of streams
of bluets and rose-mallow unfurled
across the knowes," he said as nurses
held a poultice to her shuddering ribs.
In murmurs the wind presided
over a mutinous dawn.
She asked if the mining was
complete on the ridge below,
or if the stones would conquer them
like tiny falling planets.

The hour steered away; her
hollow pace became a small charity.
Then her George could only recall
to himself the honey-scented river and
the day he had adored her birthmark
as they pondered over dappled maps
of blue and gold. At last, he smoothed her
crown of plaiting—this, his great inheritance.

A GIFT: NOUVEAU EGG CUP
FROM MUNICH

Its card reads "New *and* Functional" in 1911,
and the silver-footed womb, licked with
sordid petals and whiplash lines finely pearled

leaves room for an egg which does not sit or stand
but reclines into its calming lapse of curve.

What ecstatic possibilities one early day

for the woman who decided to serve her love
and pretended shamefully, just for a second,
to be from Vienna
              letting her wrap fall from her shoulder.
She set at his place, overlapped
with the morning-tree's shadows, the cup—

this little death-bed for yellow-gold—

knowing, of course, that breakfast together
was farther than the slow rhythms of fruit.

So treasure, my *own* love, this blessing with tea.

BELATED PALMS AND ORCHIDS

"Never let your daughter keep a black cat
        or she will surely
        never marry"—the proverb told,
so she put it to a tune and sang it
to the top of the stairs.
        "Look, I was ruthless," she said,
propping the album, "in my strapless
black maillot." The water was caught
        around her ankles as if she'd just
dropped her skirt. Ahead of her
a coronation of waves, eye-deep

and decked with exclamations of fish.
        Where else would she convene
        in her lemon-tree years?
Still another fitting: she turned me
in an embrace of blue tulle and reached
        for one more pearl-headed pin.
We both tacked on the small cordate leaves
and dripping sequins, and after
        several poses, I feigned banishment
behind a cottage front
with the shutters painted on

and put my powdered white arms
        through the windows.
        Not to go on without more tea,
she brought the kettle from the stove,
"for the weak-humored, like me."
        We took our break on the porch
and viewed the yard
as she called out the ailing plants
        in need of her attention; and I believe
as her tea steeped, she looked
at the scene painted on her cup

and wished she were that small—
            pagodas, bamboo, and a boat
            from which her friends waved;
a moon canopied their evening ride.
Through another hazed blue,
            along this bone-colored sand, now,
I can't find the green spectacles
that were sorted so evenly around
            that early yard.
She renamed its atmosphere,
"scented ennui" and "our season

of bleeding plums" because beyond it
            (for her) there was an ocean just
            overlaid with garden.
By the avenues of streamers and puppeteers
carnival lights
            stitched the dark gulf waters,
and she, dazzled by its strangeness
and her own recollections,
            described a few
of her more passionate acquaintances.
Weary of our battery of costumes,

often, in the late hours
            before shutting down the sprinklers,
            we had our sherbert-finish
as she repeated her formula
of me: "You consist of impatience
            with a toe-full of indifference,
too ready to ruin!"
She sneered at my costumes, never looking
            at me, "That Tchaikovsky-trimming,
and *so* contagious." She faded, then began
all over about an old husband

who "snored like some half-beast
      content with his conspiracies,"
      and the houses she'd once created.
She hoped I'd covet her worries
and calamities, but I sought
      another breed of luxury
alien to melancholy.
Long afterwards she described to me
      that dust-grey, early dawn of summer,
her empty house that felt as though
it had been pillaged, her joyless fatigue,

her dress with its beaded front,
      and the uneasy cats summoned home
      by her voice and the night.
Sometimes I expect to see her sitting here
by the beach, oblivious
      to the cyclists on the boardwalk,
as she once sat humoring me,
ruffled and clumsy in my search
      for egg-jewels
under the foaming azaleas. How victorious
she'd be, clad in her orchid print,

shaded by the palms. She'd be alone
      with her four o'clock sympathies
      blowing gently
towards her cup. Steam rising
from her tea, a white scarf
      lost in the litanies of her hair.

VIGNETTE

She stood holding a watering can.
His father rode in from hunting
carrying a warm quail,
a seed still in its beak.

The boy sat across from her.
A skein of red wool lay
like open wings across his wrists.
She wound the yarn
around a bent card.

Cherry blossoms fell
into the folds of her apron.
He looked at the tips of branches
against the sky
and saw nothing in place.

BLACK TULIPS

1. On the Creation of Certain Appearances

Then, in an especially small August evening
as you were caught in the closeness
it occurred to you: she'd fallen from the suburbs
into the nightfishing city. Within
its streaked walls you were brought together,
done in by a certain pitch and aquatic voices.

She swore the neon words filled themselves
and hung suspended in a glassy sky.
There was an art to her smugness,
and to the black tulips placed on her doorstep
as warning, *Don't follow, Don't follow me.*
You were led through the foyer, as she, moving ahead,

quenched herself with an unseen dialogue.
Adrift on her nightmare of grandeur,
she could say each visit was only another rehearsal,
while the soft lipstick of her careful decision
concealed the elegiac pleasure you now see
as all she can claim for herself.

2. Nightshades

She imagines his compliments as stained light
heightened considerably on the parquet floor
as it displays plaids and crosses.
She's explained the concerto in the backyard
wasn't for them—all that blooming during the night
and a measure of wintergreen, a stringy trail of ivy.

She looks into white clusters of the centerpiece,
"I see no future in them. They're too content
with their stubbornness, their avid openness.
When I blow on them, they spin,
too delighted to scatter." He comes to recognize
the potion she's spilled over these few long months.

She tries on her impervious expression, then another,
lifts a beaded mask to her face, proclaiming,
"The Secret Society adjourns outside."
She pivots him by his shoulders toward her windowbox
of silky heads, "These are our double lives,"
and pushes the shutters to a dark morning.

3. Renaissance Woman in Cahoots with The Prime Mover

I'd not counted on such miracles of propriety
and thought twice of offering my surprise
when we first met. You knew the phase
I was going through and let the salmon-colored
petals fall lusciously on the carpet
and for once, my body could not keep up.

On the balcony we were served together—
a steaming soup and a platter of cold meats.
I miss our scandalous afternoons marked
by a few sisterly disturbances.
I had begun to read right through you,
as you pointed out the Four Winds.

I, too, had those fantasies of black rain,
the particular chemistry of it, how it could nurture
hybrids like ourselves. What holds your voice now?
Anxious again for your bird-like frivolities—
I am suddenly much too alone
with my earth and its doily of stars.

AFTER ESTRANGEMENT

You should know the kind
of morning it is—
one gods have argued over for years.

But I've decided I'm under
a Byzantine curse out of which endings
situate themselves
like deep forests.

The players are strewn
in the empty heart
of a house.
She's called up her lost cat
who kept her comfortable
when the weather wouldn't.
His promises are like an addict's;
they hang camouflaged
in the lying air.
They both bend close
to a package of undone letters.
(Remember, I've a knack for detecting
in those faint, desirous courtyards
where love once happened.)

You've argued for your eloquent society,
your chronic politics,
yet still you're fazed
by your worldly withdrawals
because the whole of us
can't seem to make you gloomy enough.

I take to the armchair
and look at the two of them from here.
They're out of step, gothic.
I've always cherished the dark rivers
of what's unfashionable.

Even the fireplace is complicit
as it gives up its last bouquets.
She wants one to hold
against him and the room's operas.

As sure as you held the moon
in your perverse opal,
their outcome is apparent.
Their planned departure is just
ahead of them: she'll harness
the gentle ribs of her cat
and leave in her most unseasonable dress.

What nonsense.
They only want to starve their history,
watch it dwindle
against the southeast light.
A shame—they'd seemed so sea-worthy.

Now, as voyaging linens precede
the stairs, the morning lingers
like trouble,
and they nod off.
The troubadours, too,
have neglected them.
Who can help them
to summon the illusion of desire?

ACKNOWLEDGEMENTS

American Poetry Review: "The Visitation"
American Voice: "Belated Palms and Orchids"
The Antioch Review: "Black Tulips"
Carolina Quarterly: "Invitations to Spring: Letters with Elizabeth"
Crazyhorse: "Laughter and Diamonds"
The Denver Quarterly: "Letter," "A Painter of Destinies"
The Georgia Review: "Conversation with Isadora Duncan"
The Jacaranda Review: "Conversation with Eva Hesse"
The Journal: "Ballad of Peaches"
The Little Magazine: "Conversation with Frida Kahlo"
The Missouri Review: "Conversation with Mary Cassatt"
Ploughshares: "After Estrangement"
Quarry West: "Five Masques for the Body"
Western Humanities Review: "Waiting," "Pavlova: Elements of Evening"

I would like to thank the Maryland Arts Council for a grant which aided in the completion of this manuscript.

Some of these poems also appeared in the chapbook *Black Tulips* published in 1990 by Haw River Books.

NOTES

CONVERSATION WITH MARY CASSATT:
Cassatt and Her Circle: Selected Letters, Nancy Moull Mathews, ed.

WAITING:
Waiting for God, Simone Weil, translated by Emma Crauford.

BELATED PALMS AND ORCHIDS:
Sido, Colette, translated by Enid McLeod.

ABOUT THE AUTHOR

Molly Bendall was born in Richmond, Virginia. She trained and performed as a ballet dancer, and later received a B.A. from Virginia Intermont College and graduate degrees in English/Creative Writing from the University of Virginia and the Johns Hopkins University. She currently teaches at the University of Southern California in Los Angeles.

THE PEREGRINE SMITH POETRY SERIES

Christopher Merrill, General Editor

Sequences, by Leslie Norris
Stopping by Home, by David Huddle
Daylight Savings, by Steven Bauer
The Ripening Light, by Lucile Adler
Chimera, by Carol Frost
Speaking in Tongues, by Maurya Simon
The Rebel's Silhouette, by Faiz Ahmed Faiz
        (translated by Agha Shahid Ali)
The Arrangement of Space, by Martha Collins
The Nature of Yearning, by David Huddle
After Estrangement, by Molly Bendall